Jump Seat Leadership

The guide to informal
leadership in the fire service

Joshua S. Chase

Published By: Joshua S. Chase
JoshChase.org
Cover Design: Joshua S. Chase
Edited By: Nealy Gihan
purpleinked.com
ISBN: 9798590489589

DEDICATION

To all the men and women who aspire to be leaders in the fire service. You know who you are.

CONTENTS

ACKNOWLEDGMENTS

I guess I have to acknowledge my first crew at Station Two. Learned a lot and still learning. Thanks Brandon.

INTRODUCTION

Leadership at the informal level is becoming a lost art in the fire service. As on-the-job experience slowly retires and times change, we lack leaders in the firehouse. Not officers and managers, but leaders. We lack men and women who are willing to set the example and lead from the jump seat. We need people who are eager to serve the public in a standard way beyond just doing their job. Leaders who influence and motivate others to rally around them bring a whole new level of public service to the public we took an oath to serve.

Have you ever been stationed at a firehouse without a leader? I'm not talking about an officer; I'm talking about a leader. It sucks. No one has any real direction. They come to work, do their job, and go home. There is no one to care for, lead, or make the crew better.

Leaders take people places. They lead them there. If there is no leader, there's a pretty good chance of you and your crew getting stuck right where you are. Atmospheres without leadership create a stagnant environment that rages against all progress.

This is what jump seat leadership is all about. Leading from your current position no matter what it says on your shirt or what kind of badge you have. Firefighters, paramedics, and EMT's can all lead. This isn't you replacing your officer; it's you supporting your officer and administration in leading and developing the crews at your firehouse. It's choosing to be part of the solutions and stop complaining about the problems. This decision we make to lead starts long before we even think about getting promoted.

We must stop waiting until promotional exams to consider the magnitude of what it takes to lead. Unfortunately, some of us will never pick up a book or take a class on leadership. We will wait until right before a promotional exam to even crack a book. Then after we get promoted, we never do anything to better ourselves as leaders. Erroneous.

Make no mistake. A promotion doesn't make you a leader. It merely puts you in a position of leadership. Being the leader your crew deserves is up to you. You may have earned the title, but it doesn't instantly make you a leader.

Especially if you've done nothing to prepare yourself to lead.

Preparing yourself to lead at the informal level starts now — today. Suppose you don't establish yourself as an informal leader in your department now. In that case, you will be behind the eight ball when and if you get promoted someday. You don't have to play catch up when the opportunity to step up and lead is right in front of you.

Until I got promoted, I made a career of leading at the informal level. Not because I wanted to, it's just kind of how things ended up. For almost fifteen years, I'd been a firefighter. Before that, I was a sergeant in the U.S. Army. Up until then, I'd never been an officer, lieutenant, captain, or chief. I was just a good old Jake riding in the jump seat. I had taken the promotional exam a few times but never did that well. I watched most of my close buddies get promoted and move on to bigger and better things. While I'd just come to work every day and ride in the back.

As my career progressed naturally, I learned more, did more, and experienced more. I've always had a deep motivation to lead and feel like I have something to offer. I thought I had to be an officer to lead. Then one day, I realized something. That's not true.

Getting promoted would put me in a leadership position, but that wouldn't make me a leader. I had to foster my own leadership culture. I had to learn to lead from where I was without a promotion or title. I had to find a way to do it without a bugle on my collar while still being respectful of the leadership that's in place.

So that's what I've done. I've found holes and filled gaps that needed leadership. I've brought fresh ideas and new perspectives to things, and most days it was received well.

If there was a rookie to train, I took him in.

If there was training that needed doing, I stepped up. I did everything I could think of to lead at the informal level and help my officer and crew.

Most of the bosses I've worked for have been appreciative, and it's taken a lot off their plate. Others, not so much. They've seen it as a threat to stage a coup and take over. If that was the case, I just backed off.

The point is if you feel called to lead, do it. Do it right now. Don't wait. Not everyone feels the call to lead. So, if you feel like the person, let's get it done.

The words on these pages are going to help you get started at leading right where you are. Some of these things you might already be doing. Great. Keep at it. If you're reading this, it's because you want help and are making the decision to lead long before a promotion.

An informal leader is a man or woman who doesn't have the official title or authority to lead the crew. However, the crew follows this person anyway. The following chapters will help you in your journey of leading from the jump seat in the fire service.

Jump Seat Leadership

CHAPTER ONE
NO ONE CARES

I started my career with the fire service in July 2005. I was stoked. I applied, went through the application process, and got picked up in about six months with Norfolk Fire Rescue. I jumped into the academy headfirst. I loved this stuff.

When I applied, I had already been serving in the U.S. Army National Guard as a helicopter crew chief. So, I'd already been to U.S. Army basic training. I wasn't too worried about the academy and what it entailed. It was put up, shut up, have fun, and play the game.

So that's what I did. I did that until the Army gave me orders to go to Iraq right in the middle of the fire academy. My Army unit heard rumors we might be getting deployed, but now it was real. I notified my fire instructors, and in October 2005, I took a military leave of absence. I left the academy and headed for war. Good times. By the time it was all said and done, I didn't return to the fire academy until May 2007. Later that year, I finished up the academy and hit the street with Norfolk Fire Rescue in October 2007.

One thing I learned on the street very quickly: I didn't know anything. I had just been to war with one of the best aviation battalions in the Army. I flew in some cool missions and got to do some badass stuff. All that said, guess what? I didn't know anything when it came to the fire service, and no one cared about my military career.

This was the fire service, not the Army, and I was starting from square one.

It took about three days on the street, and I caught my first fire at a candy factory not far from my station, Station Two. I literally followed my captain around like a lost puppy that day. I had no idea what was going on. We showed up, and it was chaos to me back then. Smoke, fire, hose lines, running, people yelling. At one point while getting the hose line ready, I accidentally opened the bale and sprayed my captain in the face with water. He was too focused to even notice, but I did. I was a complete mess.

The candy factory fire was a good fire. It was in a cut-up commercial building in an industrial area. We dragged a two-and-half-inch hose line into zero visibility while machines were still running, and I sprayed water at a fire I couldn't see. Aside from having the aid of a thermal imaging camera, we were essentially blind once we entered the smoke. The hose line worked me like a summer job that day. The captain had a senior guy come up and take the hose line from me. Also, I think I sucked down all the air in my tank in about six minutes.

My captain told me to head out back to the truck when my tank was low. This added to my chaos. I got on the hose line and followed it out until I didn't. I somehow came off the hose line and got a little lost. Well, I thought I was lost. My captain was right behind me with some "kind words" to steer me back to the hose line. At some point, we were all back outside near the truck. My head was spinning, I was tired, and I thought we were done. It was right about that time my captain, who said he never yells during fires, was yelling at me to grab a new bottle. We were going back in as soon as they needed us. We got new tanks and eventually got back to work. I somehow ended up on the roof on a hose line while other companies put a trench cut in the building. I remember looking over and seeing another captain walking around the roof with his jacket open, no tank, smoking a cigarette, while supervising his company performing work. I'm sure that's not policy, but I thought it was badass, and he's retired anyway.

We were at that fire for the better part of the day. I think it stayed at two alarms but could have gone to three. I didn't know and don't remember. I was a rookie, and like I said, I didn't know anything. That night I switched over to ride the ambulance, and we got toned out for another big fire in our district. I mostly got to watch operations, hand out water, and do rehab stuff. What a great day. My third day on the job and I was just handed a pretty nice welcome to the fire service.

I could tell you a few stories, but so could any fireman who's done a few things.

There's one reason I chose this story. That day no one asked me what Army unit I served in, how many medals I had, what my rank in the army was, or how many soldiers I had under me. They didn't want to know about combat, flight time, or weapons qualification. They didn't care, and it didn't matter. I was now a member of the fire service, and it was time to learn the job.

My career and reputation in the Army didn't transfer over, and I don't think it should have. This was a new kind of job, a new enemy, new supervisors, and different challenges. No one cared about what I had done and where I came from. They expected me to learn my job, get good at it, and be a fireman, whatever that looked like. This job came with standards, customs, and traditions, and I was now a part of that.

When I say no one cares, I mean it. They probably care about you as a person, but they really don't care about what job you came from. We only care if you care enough to learn this job. We have a job to do, and some of us take it seriously. My captain was serious and made sure I knew my job. I never said dumb things like "well in the army…" I kept my mouth shut, gave him the respect he earned, and did my best to listen.

Not all true. I talked a lot and failed on several occasions to listen. But six years later when I left my first captain's command, I was set up for a career full of success. He made sure I was good to go.

In this job, you must earn the trust of the men and women around you. Keep what you've done before the fire service in your back pocket. You'll need it, but not right away. Your reputation starts the first day you walk into the academy. What you've done before this doesn't matter as far as your reputation, but you can apply the skills you have learned outside of the fire service to help you along the way. Once you've got a solid base of knowledge on the job, someone might start to care. But for now, they probably don't. Don't take it to heart. I don't think there's anything wrong with having to prove yourself in certain lines of work. The fire service is one of them. We save lives here; we don't flip burgers. No disrespect if you do, burgers are delicious.

One of the hardest things I've learned about jump seat leadership is that you start from the bottom. You listen a lot, grab as much knowledge as possible, and apply it in the right areas. A lot of us will spend most of our careers as guys riding in the jump seat. Lights and sirens always blazing, doing the speed limit, to the fire scene to do a job that we love, and that's OK.

One of the main principles I want to get across in this book is that you don't need a bugle to lead. You can lead right where you're at. It's going to take a lot of work, a little passion, and some company pride. But you can get it done and be good at it. I haven't done it all right. In fact, I've probably done more wrong. But I believe that I have tried to be the best informal leader that I know how to be over the years. It took a senior guy to straighten me out from time to time, but I've gotten it done.

You don't have to be a new guy to get this principle. Whether you have six months or fifteen years on the job, you can still lead from the jump seat. So many of us wait until we have a title or position to start leading and influencing others. I mean, hell, some of you know people right now who are in charge who are not leading. They're probably great managers, but if no one follows them, they're not leading. Don't let your fire company suffer due to someone else's lack of leadership. Step up, fill the gap, and learn to lead from the jump seat.

CHAPTER TWO
ACQUIRE KNOWLEDGE

To lead from the jump seat, you're going to need a good base knowledge of how the fire service works. In my earlier years in the fire service, I didn't have much firefighter and emergency response knowledge. Aside from the academy and some military first aid training, my knowledge of what to do in certain situations was slim. I knew absolutely nothing about the fire department when I applied. I legitimately just wanted to help people, and the fire service seemed like a good place to do it.

I took it upon myself to be fully engaged in the culture of the fire service. I considered myself a leader, even as a rookie, but that didn't mean I spoke up all the time. Sometimes being a leader means learning how to acquire knowledge and follow orders when given. That was the focus in my earlier years of the fire service. I wanted to soak up everything I could about this job.

My captain liked to train regularly back then. There weren't many days through the shift cycle that we didn't train. Some days it was stretching lines, and others it was street drills. Even on our "no training" days, we still went around to hydrants in our first due and inspected them. We would stop at a set number of hydrants and test each one, making sure they were accessible and that we could get caps off with ease. Then we would eventually start talking about GPM's, water flow, and other water supply topics. So technically, we were training.

When we weren't doing official training, we were doing our own training around the galley table. We discussed scenarios, apparatus placement, and department policies. Then after dinner, we would grab a cup of coffee and watch YouTube videos of house fires from other counties and discuss size ups, strategy, and tactics. I mean, I breathed this stuff. My whole crew did. I was fully engaged in my job because I knew I needed knowledge.

All this training I'm talking about took place between calls. There was plenty of on the job training as well. I was assigned to a busy engine company back then. We were also getting to put our skills into practice and put our training to use. Don't get me wrong. It's not like we caught a fire every day because we didn't. However, we had enough that we could put our training to the test and develop a good base knowledge of what an aggressive engine company should look like.

When I wasn't at work, I was in the books. I enrolled in a local community college and began to pursue a degree in fire science. I watched videos at home, read fire magazines and books. I'm telling you, I was all in. I knew I was a leader and wanted to be able to have a positive influence in fire service. I also knew I couldn't do that without having a good base knowledge of what this job entailed.

I also took classes that were offered. Thankfully, the state I work in provides a ton of free fire classes that only require me to sacrifice time. Over the years, I have taken advantage of several classes that would help me along the way in my career. If you are young, single, childless, and in the fire service; this is the time to take as many classes as you can! I've always had a wife and kids, so classes have been challenging. But I have still tried to take courses that I really felt would help me in the long run. There are also a lot of paid classes you can take part in that are all over the country. It's worth it if you're considering stepping up and leading from the jump seat.

I don't care how you get it or where you get it from, but you must find a way to learn whatever you can about this job. There are so many resources out there these days. You don't have to know everything, but you need to know something.

Jump Seat Leadership

CHAPTER THREE
EXPERIENCE NEEDED

Knowledge is great, but without experience it doesn't carry a lot of weight. Reading ten books about putting out a fire doesn't match up to being inside a burning building, searching for victims, and executing a successful rescue. I grabbed a lot of knowledge in my first few years as a firefighter but had no experience. I thought I knew a whole lot, and I did. I had a lot of book knowledge, but nowhere near the number of years of experience it takes to speak up about anything.

And sometimes when talking about experience in the fire service, it's still not about your years of experience. Depending on your department's size, you may have stations scattered all over your municipality. We all respond to different districts. We all have a few small houses in the city that just don't run as many calls as other houses. It is what it is. While those guys may have years on the job, they don't have a lot of experience.

When I say experience, I'm talking about on the job and performing the work. I'm not talking about the guy that has been at the slow house for fifteen years and makes a killer beef stew. He's probably a nice guy, but by default, he's probably only been to a handful of real calls.

This is when people say, "Well, that's not his fault." Yes, it is. You want experience, right? Ask for a transfer. You know damn well there are busier firehouses in your city, and you could probably easily get to one. Now if you just happen to work somewhere where it's not busy, I guess I can't offer you a lot of help here.

You get the point, though. Years on the job and experience are two different things. Set yourself up for success. You want to lead from the jump seat before you get promoted someday? You need to position yourself to gain experience throughout your career as a firefighter. Don't settle at a slow house with guys that don't care. Find like-minded people that do care. Pick their brain. When there is training, step up and volunteer. Training is the best place to make mistakes.

When you get the knowledge, find ways to gain experience in the areas you just studied. For you, this may mean a transfer or switching fire departments. It's all in how much you are willing to put into the job. Just don't blame anyone else for your lack of experience and opportunity. You're most likely a letter away from a new firehouse. If that's what you want.

I feel like it's pretty cut and dry. Experience comes with doing and performing this job. Sure, some years you may be sharper than others, but do what you can to stay as sharp as you can. I know a few guys that have been at busy houses for five years and guys that have been at slow houses for fifteen. Who do you think has more experience? Who do you want in your house when it's lit off? The guy who has been in the fire service longer, or the guy who has performed on the job longer? You can do your own math on that one.

CHAPTER FOUR
MATURITY COUNTS

Seems a little weird to me that I'm writing a section on maturity. As I write this, I'm thirty-seven years old, still have a lot of life ahead of me, and a lot of growing up to do. But I can say I am more mature now than I was years ago. I'm probably not where I need to be, but I have made some progress. I just believe that knowledge and experience can only go so far without maturity to accompany them.

Knowledge is the acquisition of wisdom in a subject matter area. Experience is when you get to see the knowledge or wisdom in action. Maturity should be right on its heels. Maturity in the fire service is the ability to know when to apply the knowledge and experience you have to a given situation. It's knowing when to speak up. It's also knowing when to shut up and sit down. Maturity is a hard lesson to learn for most of us, and I've had many humbling experiences along the way. I have also had to do a lot of apologizing.

One thing I have realized about maturity is that it takes time. It doesn't matter how bad you want it and how much knowledge or experience you have. It takes time for all three of these things to meld together. I can remember acquiring as much knowledge as I could, getting a little experience, and then thinking I was good to go. When I had about five years in the fire service, I thought I was hot shit. Still, I lacked a level of maturity that would carry the weight of my knowledge and experience.

For the most part, I would say my whole crew was like that back then. Or at least most of us. We gave our company officer a run for his money and made him earn his money every day while we were on shift. We were a bunch of young, hardheaded guys who thought we had it all together. We were good at what we did, but we lacked the maturity for anyone to take us seriously. We put up, but we also spoke up. We said what we wanted to, when we wanted to say it, and didn't really want to hear it from anyone. We eventually got nicknamed "the arrogant assholes." We embraced it and kept driving forward. We were good at what we did, and we told everyone.

A lot of this was the love for the job and company pride, but we could have found a more mature way to go about it some days. We were the fire service kind of guys who scored a touchdown and did a ten-minute dance. I would say we've all matured some since then and would now just put the ball in the end zone and go back to the bench.

Knowledge, experience, and maturity all go hand in hand. They might not even go in order, but I think they are all required if you want to lead when you're not in charge. You want your leadership to take you seriously and be able to trust you. At this stage in my career, I have bosses who aren't worried about me and another fireman tackling a fire interior while he takes command outside. I've developed a good base of knowledge, I have the experience, and I am mature enough to make the right decisions.

You may have the knowledge and experience, but if you're a younger firefighter on the job, give it some time.

CHAPTER FIVE
YOUR OFFICER NEEDS YOU

You may not think so, but your officer needs you, and you need to make yourself available to be used. If you want to lead from the jump seat, just lead. If you've been in the fire service long enough, you have probably seen some incompetent leaders. Every day, things come out of their mouth at morning roll call, and you can't believe this guy is in charge.

Unfortunately, what I've done in some cases is just rolled with it most days and talked about what I would change if I were in charge. After line up all the guys and girls go to their corners and talk about how crazy line up sounded ... again. They might be right. But what are they going to do to fix it? Probably nothing.

It's much easier to continue to complain about a problem than to address it and make a change. Often, if we can't solve the whole problem, we won't even try fixing it. Maybe you only have part of the solution. Give it a shot. Really anything. The important thing is to do something.

Hell, your officer might be stoked for you to step up and lead. Now they can keep watching the latest Netflix series on their iPad while you train the guys. He probably had no intention to pick up and lead anyway. Someone needs to make sure the men and women at your house have a clue when it comes to serving the public. Stop waiting on someone else to do it. You do it. Chances are you're already thinking thoughts like "When I get promoted..."

Why wait until you get promoted? What can you put into place now that will prepare you for promotion?

Some officers are terrible leaders because they honestly just don't care. Not all of them, but they're out there. If you work for an officer that doesn't seem to care, they probably won't care about you stepping up and taking a leadership role. Use the opportunity of an officer that doesn't care to give yourself some experience leading. Stop using the fact that they don't care as an excuse for you not to care. The time to prepare yourself to do their job one day is now. If you foster an attitude of not caring now, it will be a bad habit to break when the guys are now looking to you as an officer to lead.

Now I've had all kinds of leaders in the fire service and my time in the Army: leaders who cared, didn't care, or just cared too much. I have not always stepped in when I should have. There have been multiple occasions when I've decided to adopt the "I just work here" mentality. Knowing that I work for someone who doesn't care and who doesn't pay me to care more than they do. Here's the thing that I discovered for myself: They do pay me to care more than he or she does.

Fact is, I work for a paid department, and we're all paid to care and expected to adopt and follow our department's core values. If he or she doesn't adopt and care about these core values, it's still my job, regardless if I agree with them or not. Even if you don't have the title and position, it doesn't mean you aren't allowed to care.

Be the informal leader in your firehouse. Be the go-to guy for the officer and your crew. Be the guy who your peers see as worth paying attention to and following. If you know your officer needs help, volunteer to take things off his or her plate. Make life easy for him or her. You can only hope that someone would do this for you someday.

It's a lot easier to sit back and watch someone fail at work. In the back of your head, you can tell yourself that if there is a big screw up, you had nothing to do with it. Not true. If something is screwed up and you did nothing to help or address the situation, you did have something to do with it. You may not end up in a chief's office over it, but you do have to sleep at night.

We need to be the kind of firefighters that step up and fill the gaps in our leadership. Not ones who shy away from responsibility. We all have a responsibility to make sure we go home safe at the end of our shift.

If you work for an officer who seems to be drowning, reach out and help pull them out of the water. Throw them a lifeline. You can probably see the areas they are lacking in, and you or the guys in the firehouse might be stronger in those areas. There is nothing wrong with stepping up to help your officer be successful. If you know your officer sucks at setting up training, set up some training. I could insert a million examples here.

Sidebar: There are assholes out there you won't be able to help. They are stubborn, hardheaded, and dont give a shit about what you think. In that case, my advice would be to set an example for the rest of your guys by doing the right thing when you can and lay low. Do not go head-to-head with this guy. There is no point. Stand up for the things you must, but do not pick every battle. You will end up frustrated and probably transferred. Sometimes you have to suck it up and move on. If you can't take it, ask for a transfer. Chances are you're not the only one that sees what's going on. However, you might be the only one that cares.

CHAPTER SIX
THE MIRROR

You can't lead from the jump seat unless you are willing to look in the mirror. You must be able to identify your own flaws and bad habits and be willing to face and change them. Maybe not right away. We can't change overnight. But it might be time to make some changes.

You can't really lead from the jump seat if you haven't learned how to lead yourself. You may be looking around thinking that you could do things better and make better decisions, but what are you doing to lead yourself? What are your standards and core values? Do you even have any that guide your everyday decisions?

This is probably one of the things we don't like to do. We love to point out the flaws of others. But if you're going to lead anyone anywhere, you have to be able to take responsibility for yourself.

There have been many times in my career that not being squared away had prevented me from saying something when I needed to. I can only hold others to the same standard I hold myself to. I can't expect others to go above and beyond if I'm not willing to.

I would ask you if you're even willing to take responsibility for where you're at in the fire service? If you're not, then the tools in this book are useless. They require you to look in the mirror, and some of us just aren't ready to do that. I can't talk to others about being on time if I'm always late. Or ask guys to tuck in their shirts if mine's untucked.

In leading yourself, you must decide what's important to you. Mainly because you cannot excel at everything. You can make an effort at everything, but you can't be an expert at it all. What's important to you? What do you want to be known for?

For me, it's on the job skills and physical training. Those are two things I see as crucial to my career and the citizens I serve. In leading myself, I make sure I stay physically fit and I know how to do my job when I get on scene. You won't see me barking at anyone a whole lot about housework, cooking, or washing the trucks. I just want you to be able to do your job. My life and the life of citizens depend on those we work with.

I don't give a shit if you can push a broom or mop the floor. That's not what we got hired for. Those things have to get done, but they shouldn't take priority over what we took an oath to do — protect life and property.

Where do you need to lead yourself right now? What areas can you improve in? I'm telling you, looking in the mirror and owning your current situation is huge. The first thing that's going to happen if you start leading from the jump seat is people will get on the hater train. They will check out every inch of what you do and how you're doing it. They are looking for something wrong with you.

Don't worry about it. Own it. If someone points out something, humble yourself and try to fix it. Plus, you will inspire change in other people. Habits are attractive, good or bad. Whether you believe it or not, most times when you are leading yourself, you are leading other people. Whether you like it or not.

I had a habit for a little while of checking off

the trucks in the morning and not filling out the check-off sheet all the way. My logic was that I'd checked it off so it was all good. And then I would go and make breakfast. I'm not proud of it, but I'm being honest. My job wasn't done. Most days, I'd just let the junior guy to me get the clipboard. But when he forgot it or it wasn't completed, it was on me. Not only should I have just been doing it, I was also setting a bad example to the rookie of how things get done. There's probably a guy out there now who's doing it the wrong way, and I'm to blame.

One day the captain brought all the check-off sheets in from the month prior and mentioned most of them not being done on the days we worked. He addressed the whole crew and politely asked us to make sure it didn't happen again. Well, my buddy did some investigative work and went back and looked at the schedule to see who was riding the truck those days. It was me. I didn't really argue much. I fessed up. I didn't really have a good reason to justify it either. I just apologized and told them it wouldn't happen again. Which it probably did until it didn't.

We all have areas we can work on. Leading from the jump seat means taking the time to look in the mirror and make the necessary changes so that when others look at you, they see the kind of firefighter they want to be.

Now, forget the mirror. I know, you just read a whole section about looking in the mirror and owning your shit. Well, forget it for a second. For most of us, we've already had the opportunity to look in the mirror. We know we are lazy in some areas and have flaws that are way beyond fixing tomorrow. We have developed complacent habits that will one day get us or the guy next to us hurt. What do we do about it? The time for self-evaluation is over. Time to ask others.

One of the most honest places I have ever worked is the firehouse. Firefighters are, for the most part, honest about the people they work with. If you want a straight-up real answer about where you are at in the fire service, ask someone. Ask the guy in the jump seat next to you what he thinks when he sees your name on the roster with him. You know exactly what I'm talking about because you've done it.

Whether it's the shift prior or the morning of, most guys look at the roster and know who they are on the truck with the next day. As soon as you see that certain name, you already know what kind of day you're going to have. If you've never done this or never thought this, you might be the guy no one wants to ride with.

When you're asking for advice or input, don't ask a guy who you know won't give you a real opinion. Ask a guy who you know will give a down and dirty answer.

Ask him to identify areas that he thinks you can work on and improve in. Even in reading this, most of you know who you need to talk to. Peer evaluation is extremely effective if you are willing to do something with the feedback. You may have already been pulled aside by your peers or a senior guy. How did you react? Did you fix it? Or did you shrug him off because you think he was wrong.

I've been pulled aside multiple times in my career by guys who were senior to me. For the most part, I have taken their advice. But not all the time. I often neglected to swallow my pride and just continued to do what I wanted to do.

This one time, I didn't realize that this guy was going out of his way to make sure I understood something that he had gotten years ago. He saw the gift of informal leadership in my career and addressed the fact that I was not living up to what I knew

I had in me. I was pissed. I was pissed because he called me out and I was at a place in my career where I had a good base knowledge of the job. I didn't want to help lead anyone. I wanted to lay low and just do my job. But he saw what the crew needed and knew that I had the potential to help lead the men.

If I'm honest, I was threatened by his level of informal leadership and seniority. I thought I had things under control until I learned that he was in control. So instead of being respectful and taking the advice in good stride, I fought him on it, and we bumped heads from there on out. Remember earlier when I addressed maturity? I wish I could say that this incident was in the first couple years of my career, but it wasn't. I had been in the department fourteen years at this point. I'm a work in progress just like you.

Well, one day it came to a head, and we

were literally face to face in the galley at lunch. My young arrogant pride had boiled over, and he'd had enough. We had words and did not have any words for the next month or so until we both couldn't sleep over it and finally squashed it. Nothing like a good old bit of station drama!

When I finally sucked it up and apologized, all he said was, "Thanks man. Just take the next step."

He was talking about informal leadership to formal leadership. He was telling me to put some effort into the promotional exam. He saw something I didn't see in the mirror. He also saw things I didn't want him to see.

I've been lucky. I've had guys who have cared enough to pull me aside and give me advice when I needed it. And when they don't offer it, I ask for advice and see what other people think. Ask your peers what they think of you, your work ethic, and the way you carry yourself around the firehouse. For the most part, I think you will get some honest answers.

Then once you get those answers, try to work on them. Go back to those men or women and say thank you. Ask them how they think you are doing. Ask them to hold you accountable for getting better. Leading has a lot to do with looking in the mirror and learning how to lead yourself. But when the mirror isn't working or isn't enough, It's time to get an honest opinion.

CHAPTER SEVEN
SOLUTIONS NOT PROBLEMS

If there is one thing I enjoy at work, it's the galley table. I've had many conversations around the galley table that I wouldn't have had anywhere else. I always joke and say that we can solve the world's problems at the galley table. The galley table is where we fix the fire service.

Most times, when I get around the galley table, I do what I say I wasn't going to do on the way to work that morning—I complain. The minute line up is done, or a new rumor gets started, so does the conversation. This usually ends up with someone complaining about something or someone.

Whether it's a new policy or some new training put out, someone always has something to say, including me. I can complain with the best of them. Now in past years, I was a lot worse. I've gotten better. Now I tell myself that if I'm not willing to be part of the solution, I need to stop complaining about the problem. Solutions not problems. It's helped me keep my mouth shut on several occasions. Now if I'm not willing to put effort into it, I don't give much of an opinion out loud. I've caught myself mid-sentence a couple times with my own saying. Solutions not problems.

For the most part, we walk away from the galley table with nothing accomplished but a bunch of talk. Why not take some of that talk and do something? If you're going to start leading, why not start coming up with some solutions for problems that need to be addressed instead of complaining all the time? Start setting an example as someone who isn't being scared to share the truth and address the problem. There is probably something that you are passionate about or wish would get changed. Have you pursued change in that area or just complained about it?

We have a lot of smart people in the fire service. If we don't offer ourselves an avenue to solve problems, things may never get tackled. The administration can't handle everything and blaming them for all issues won't get us anywhere. I mean, I've seen administration make what I would call dumb decisions, but the way we handled those decisions made it even worse.

I'm going to keep this one simple. If you are going to be vocal about it, be willing to contribute some time and energy into addressing the issue and making it better. It might take some time to get your point across, but there is a future generation of firefighters who can benefit from a problem you chose to solve.

CHAPTER EIGHT
CORE VALUES

I chose to write about this one last, but I think this encompasses every other point in this book. Core values are huge. They are the things that guide and motivate us in our decision making. If you don't have any, I suggest you adopt some. I have a set of personal core values that I live by. They are closely related to my faith and how I was raised. Fortunately, if you don't have any core values, most departments have some they expect and require you to adopt upon being hired.

The problem is we just look at them as some sort of cool saying that's plastered on the fire station wall. We make no effort to make those core values a part of how we make our decisions daily.

The department I work for expects us to adopt six core values. I happen to like and agree with all of them. I apply them to fit my personality in and outside of work. I'm only going to cover my favorite three, not in any particular order. They all go hand in hand. If for some reason you don't have any here are three good ones to adopt.

Accountability

Accountability is huge. We must be willing to be held accountable for our actions. Take ownership of your decisions, whether they are good or bad. Learn and grow from them. Accountability is making the decision to be responsible. If something is right, accept the praise. If something is wrong, accept discipline and criticism. Being accountable will help you grow as a leader. If you are willing to be held accountable and others see that, it will be easier for you to hold others accountable when it comes time.

Integrity

Integrity is one of my favorites, mostly because I don't define it the way everyone else does. Most people would define it as another form of honesty. Doing the right thing when no one is looking. I don't quite see it like that. To me, integrity is the ability to hold up under pressure, the ability to not buckle under the weight of a situation and make the right decisions whether someone's looking or not.

Like ninety-nine percent of firefighters, I have a side gig that brings in extra cash. I build wood tables, benches and custom furniture. When I'm building these things, I think about the integrity of the furniture. What I'm building must hold up to what it's being used for. If I'm building a dinner table, it needs to support a different amount of weight as opposed to a bench or a coffee table. When I'm thinking about the building process, I'm thinking about the integrity of the pieces I build. When the pressure or weight mounts up, will they be able to handle the pressure or will they buckle?

When I think about integrity, that's what comes to my mind. Is what I am as a fireman and what I am becoming getting me to a place where I can handle the pressures of this job?

Will my integrity be compromised in moments because I have not chosen to build myself up with knowledge, allow myself the experiences, and grow into a state of maturity where I can make the hard decisions on scene?

Now, I'm not dismissing the other definition of integrity: doing the right thing when no one is looking. I am just bringing a new perspective to it. We make the wrong decisions when others aren't looking because we haven't built ourselves up to be confident in our abilities. If we are built strong when the pressure comes, we can make the right calls when no one is looking. Chances are that if you are reading this book, you are a firefighter. That is your occupation, career, or passion. What are you doing to make sure your integrity is not compromised?

Respect

I can't say enough about respect. I would love to say that respect is earned, but it's not in some cases. If someone gets promoted, they have earned the right to be respected by rank. Whether they have earned your respect as a person is a whole other ball game. The question with this one is how do you want others to see you? Do you want to be respected because of position seniority or because of the type of person and firefighter you are? It's up to you. When it comes to earning respect, everyone is different. You will never meet everyone's standards, but you will be able to ascertain what is important and what isn't as it pertains to earning respect from the men and women around you.

You can take those and run with them or come up with your own. Either way, you need to have some sort of core values that are guiding your decision making. It's not smart to just wing it and hope you make the right decisions. Something needs to guide your everyday decision-making process.

CHAPTER NINE
MAKING THE DECISION

OK, read the following paragraph aloud:

"I am a complacent, apathetic firefighter who settles for substandard performance. I don't want to be trained, challenged or motivated to improve my skill set. I'm tired of training and doing the same old drills repeatedly. I just want to coast through my career, watch a few movies, eat some good meals, and get off easy. I don't really want to work hard, wondering if it will pay off some day. I mean what if it doesn't? Some days the fire service is exhausting, and I just want to do my time and retire."

If you are feeling like that, it happens. If you aren't, let's not get there. I've had days where I've felt like that — more than I care to admit. Every now and then, I get these thoughts that crowd my head and try to get me to settle. For years, I avoided taking the promotional exam for lieutenant seriously because I was comfortable as a firefighter. Unfortunately, being comfortable was hurting my chances of advancement.

I was in a "no more classes, no more videos, no more tabletop discussions about water supply and tactics" kind of mood for a couple years. I just knew deep down I couldn't do that forever. I took an oath when I got hired with the fire service, and I have an obligation to fulfill it. Luckily, like I mentioned earlier, I had a senior guy help straighten me out and shake that mentality.

If you are going to be a jump seat leader, you can't settle for mediocrity. Settling for a mediocre career is doable, but who would we be helping? Not myself, and what about the guys around us? We are our best chance of getting home safe every day. Aren't we counting on each other?

If you want to understand the importance of not settling, google firefighter complacency when you get a chance. It's full of stories and situations that happened because someone settled or compromised in the firehouse or on the fire ground. It will get your attention.

It's only a matter of time before you are tempted with the opportunity to settle into the easy life at the firehouse. You're eventually going to get to a point in your career when you have enough time that you're not new. Still, you don't have enough time to be considered senior. You'll have a good base knowledge of the job and will probably perform well on most calls. Some days, the last thing you'll want to do is take the lead. I'm speaking from experience. I'm telling you; I was there right around ten years on the job. Right, wrong, or indifferent, it's where I was.

Some days, it's easier to go with the flow. However, if you want to see change, only one person is going to make it happen. The decision to lead is a process. Once you make the decision, the process starts. You're going to have to change behavior, build new relationships, and change how you respond to different things around the firehouse. There may be conversations and situations that you can't be a part of anymore.

Making the decision means standing up, being bold, and attacking the task at hand. What are you waiting for? I know right now you can name three areas in your fire department that you can make a difference in. We all have something we are good at. So here we are. You have an immediate decision to make. You can continue to settle or decide to step up and be the informal leader in your firehouse. We're not going to wait until we get promoted to do this. We're stepping up to the plate now, today.

Leaders suck it up, get off their ass, make decisions, and get things done. When something is not working, they make it work. When something needs to get done, they give it a go. Leaders do something. Being a jump seat leader means that when the bullets fly and fire rages, you aren't scared to take a bullet or run into the flames. Leaders do what must be done. And in doing so, they inspire others to step up and do the same.

Once you've made your decision, stick with it. Don't check out. Being fully engaged means to be fully occupied and give something your full attention. Engaged means staying involved in your situation. Whether it's fire training, EMS training, or physical training. You must be involved. It must become part of who you are.

Being fully engaged means intentionally positioning yourself where you can lead effectively. It involves a lot of forward thinking and planning for tomorrow. You're going to have to plan out situations and consider decisions before they present themselves. It involves keeping your thoughts engaged, as well as acting daily. This may be out of your comfort zone, but it's worth it.

You're going to have to set goals before your workday begins. Have a plan for the next day or every day. Maybe every day, you will read an SOP, train, or get in the gym. Whatever it is, set goals for yourself that will keep your head in the game. Not identifying things that keep you engaged will eventually leave you sitting around questioning everything. If you have no goals, no vision, no plan; how do you expect to stay engaged? What will motivate you to stay involved? If there is no goal or nothing to work toward, what are you even doing?

The answer is simple: nothing.

When we have vision, goals, and a clear-cut idea of where we want to go, being fully engaged becomes easier. Often, we have trouble staying engaged because we haven't figured out where we want to go. We're fully committed to a half-hearted idea.

I have been in the fire service for going on fifteen years now. When I was a younger fireman, I learned early on the importance of staying engaged. I was brand new to the job and knew absolutely nothing. I went through rookie school, learned the basics, and then got assigned to a firehouse. When I arrived at my first firehouse, I realized how much I didn't know.

In rookie school, they made it clear that this job was not about me. It was about service — serving the community and making sure we were always on top of our game. I knew from Day 1 that staying engaged was going to be a priority in this job.

When I didn't understand, I asked questions. I took classes, read books, watched videos, and trained the same drills over and over and over until I was proficient, and then I trained again. Staying engaged means being fully involved and giving it your full attention.

Staying engaged won't be easy. You are going to run into obstacles. Most of those obstacles will be the men and women you work with. Don't sweat it. This is your decision, not theirs. Let them ruin their career. Whatever you do, don't quit.
Remember that phrase "quitting is not an option"? It's garbage and one of my least favorite statements. It's fake news, and I'm not going to give you some false motivation speech that will get you nowhere.

Quitting is an option. For most of us, it's the first one we entertain when things get tough. We immediately think about how awesome it would be to just quit and bypass the whole situation. We run through scenarios, come up with plans, and sometimes take the beginning steps of quitting. As if it's realistic to think our job would never offer a challenging situation ever again. Wake up, you joined the fire service.

In order to not quit, you must acknowledge that quitting is an option. It's been an option, and it will always be an option. You just must always decide to not choose this option. There is a quitter inside of you. Accept that. It's your job to keep his mouth shut.

If there's one thing I've realized over the years, it's this: Quitting is easy. It requires little to no effort. You literally have to do nothing to quit. Don't get up for work tomorrow. You want to quit and stop all forward progress? Don't move.

I would love to say that I've done my whole fire service career up until this point and never entertained the idea of quitting. I would be lying. I've just chosen to push past those things. I've had my share of bad calls and things I couldn't shake and still lose sleep over. There are things and situations that have messed with my head a little bit and challenged the hard-core resolve that I claim to have. In my earlier years I buried these things and just took them as part of the job. Now, I process the things that challenge my mindset, talk about them with others, and get help.

Recently, I was dispatched to a bad apartment fire on a ladder company. I was the acting officer, and my crew got tasked with searching for a kid on the second floor who was still trapped. Somehow, I got separated from my crew, found the kid, and got lost on the way out with the kid. Eventually, I got him to safety before I went back in and helped put the rest of the fire out.

That kid spent the week in the hospital on a breathing machine but made a full recovery. Eventually, he stopped by the station to say thank you. That was probably the highlight of my career. It's moments like those that inspire me to keep moving and push past my thoughts of complacency and its close friend, mediocrity.

To say that nothing in this job will push you to the point when you want to quit is arrogant. You may still be at work, but I work with guys every day that quit a long time ago. You know who they are, and they know who they are. All the reasons why leadership at the jump seat level is so important. Officers don't always see what the guys see.

CHAPTER TEN
TOOLS

If you decide to take the plunge into jump seat leadership, you are going to need a plan. You are going to need some clear-cut goals and have to make some immediate decisions that may start at your next shift. So that means answering some hard questions for yourself. Answering the questions is just the beginning. It will give you a place to start. After you answer them, share with someone. Start an honest conversation about how you want to change. Here are ten questions that you need to ask yourself, ten questions to help you take the plunge:

1. Where have you become complacent on the job?

2. Are you willing to take a more active role in your firehouse?

3. What are you good at?

4. Are you able to teach other members?

5. Are you willing to ask your peers where your flaws are?

6. Does your officer know he can count on you? Or is it just assumed?

7. Are you willing to talk to your officer and take more of a leadership role at work?

8. Are you in a position to set an example in your firehouse?

9. Who are your firehouse mentors?

10. Who will hold you accountable?

Leading from the jump seat is not going to be easy. You're attempting to lead without title or position. Most people are only used to leaders that manage with title and position. This will be a foreign concept to some of the guys in your firehouse. They'll wonder why you don't just let the officers do their job. In other cases, you may have officers that aren't receptive to you trying to lead without a title. Remember, you are helping and assisting your officer, not staging a coup to overthrow him!

If you genuinely want to help, it should be received well. If you try to take over, they'll sniff it out in a heartbeat, and you'll get yourself in trouble. Some will be receptive, others, not so much. You will encounter some resistance. It's worth it. Like I said in the beginning, informal leadership is becoming a lost principle in the fire service. Some have never experienced it. Just don't quit. Once you have made the decision to step up to leadership at the jump seat level, stick with it.

Like I said earlier, most of my buddies were lieutenants, captains, and chiefs long before I was. They've all worked through the ranks and got promoted, except for me. I was still kickin' it at the jump seat level. For years, that bothered me until I realized something. I had a choice. I could lead from my current position and prepare myself for promotion someday, or I could complain and stay put. I studied my ass off, applied acquired knowledge, and secured a lieutenant job this past winter.

So now, I've moved into leadership at the formal level. I'm glad I'm here, but I've been preparing for this position long before I got promoted.

You want to lead? Great, we need you. We need you now, not when you're ready to take a test. Let's get this done. Step up and lead from the jump seat.

CONCLUSION

You can do this. You can start leading today. You may be doing it already. Don't stop. It gets frustrating and your circle of friends might get smaller, but it's worth it. The fire service is suffering from a lack of leadership on every level. I've often heard that leadership starts from the top. I will agree to disagree. While that statement has some validity, it is not excuse to not lead.

Leadership starts with you. It starts with you caring enough about the profession you chose to lead yourself and others around

you. You cannot wait for someone else to do what you know you have been called to do. Just lead. Read a book, take a class, and talk to others around you who are leading.
Team up with them and create pockets of influence that will change the fire service.

If for some reason leading isn't for you, then be a good follower. Not a push over, a follower. Leaders need good followers that buy into the vision and core values of the department. If you don't want to lead or follow, I would challenge why you are working in the fire service at all. There is no place for the middle ground. There is no place for the men and women who could care less about being good leaders or followers. There is no place for the men and women who just come to work every day with no intention of making themselves or the department better.

If you are not going to lead or follow, I would kindly ask you to step aside so the rest of us can do the job that we took an oath to do. At some point you will have to choose what kind of firefighter you will be. This may include asking yourself a simple question. Is this career for you? If it's not, that's okay. I'm sure there is a good fit out there for you somewhere.

Lastly, I would ask you that if you are here, be here. Lead yourself and others well. Maybe your intention was never to retire from the fire service. Maybe this is your part time job and you own a successful business outside the fire service. No problem. Just do us a favor. Be here while you're here. We're counting on you to have our back in the same way we have yours.

Jump Seat Leadership

ABOUT THE
AUTHOR

I have been in the fire service over fifteen years. I am a Fire Lieutenant for a paid department in Norfolk, Virginia. I'm also a combat veteran of the U.S. Army. I was a Sergeant who served as a crew chief and door gunner for black hawk helicopters in western Iraq.

I've lived a little, loved a little, lost a lot, been married, had children, been widowed, been remarried, been to war, got shot at, run into burning buildings, saved some lives, helped people on an ambulance, and received a few medals.

I have a passion for leadership and to see others lead well. Through my military service, the fire service, and my life experiences, I aim to strengthen, encourage and empower others.

RESOURCES

Keep up with everything Jump Seat Leadership on social media and over at the website! Leadership seminars based off this book are available!

JumpSeatLeadership.org

FOLLOW ON FACEBOOK

@JUMPSEATLEADERSHIP

Made in United States
Cleveland, OH
30 November 2024

11074706R00056